POWERBOATS

by Lisa Bullard

Lerner Publications Company • Minneapolis

I'd like to offer special thanks to the following individuals who so generously shared their time, knowledge, and enthusiasm: Steve Montgomery; James Pernikoff; Mark Wheeler, Board of Directors, American Power Boat Association; and Sherron Winer, Partner, Powerboat Superleague. This book is especially for Max. —LB

This book is available in two editions:
Library binding by Lerner Publications Company, a division of Lerner Publishing Group
Soft cover by First Avenue Editions, an imprint of Lerner Publishing Group
241 First Avenue North
Minneapolis, MN 55401 U.S.A.

Website address: www.lernerbooks.com

Library of Congress Cataloging-in-Publication Data

Bullard, Lisa.
    Powerboats / by Lisa Bullard.
        p.   cm. – (Pull ahead books)
    Includes index.
    Summary: An introduction to various types of racing
powerboats.
    ISBN: 0–8225–0744–7 (lib. bdg. : alk. paper)
    ISBN: 0–8225–9921–X (pbk. : alk. paper)
    1. Motorboat racing—Juvenile literature. 2. Motorboats—
Juvenile literature. [1. Motorboat racing. 2. Motorboats.]
I. Title: Power boats. II. Title. III. Series.
GV835.9.B85 2004
797.1'4—dc21   2003003562

Manufactured in the United States of America
1 2 3 4 5 6 – JR – 09 08 07 06 05 04

Some powerboats are built to race!

All powerboats have **engines.** An engine puts the power in a powerboat! Can you find the engine on the back of this boat?

There are many kinds of powerboats. Their **hulls** come in many shapes. A hull is the boat's body, the part that moves through the water.

Why would this be called a V-bottom hull?

The bottom of the hull is shaped like the letter "v." V-bottom hulls cut quickly through big waves.

How many hulls does this boat have?

Boats with two hulls are called **catamarans.** Only the thin edges of the hulls touch the water. This makes the boat glide very fast.

Tunnel boats have **sponsons** along their sides. They form a tunnel under the boat. When the tunnel boat speeds, air gets trapped in the tunnel.

The tunnel boat races. Air rushes under the boat and lifts it. Now the boat can speed faster!

Hydroplanes have sponsons on the front sides of the boat. Hydroplanes ride a cushion of air. Racing a hydroplane is almost like flying!

Unlimited Hydroplanes are the fastest powerboats. They can go over 200 miles per hour. That's as fast as a race car.

Most Unlimited Hydroplanes use turbine engines. Turbine engines are the same powerful engines used on jet airplanes.

Here is an Unlimited Hydroplane being lowered into the water. It even looks like an airplane!

Some engines have propellers on their bottoms. The propeller goes in the water. Its blades turn and move the boat.

Outboard engines are outside the boat.
This powerboat has two outboard
engines. Do you see two propellers?

Where is this powerboat's engine?

Some powerboats have their engine inside the boat. This is called an **inboard** engine.

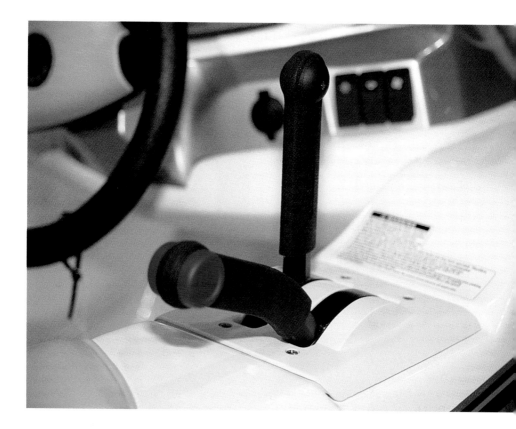

Did you know that powerboats don't have brakes? The driver controls the speed using a stick called a **throttle.**

The throttle is in the **cockpit.** That is where the driver is.

The steering wheel is in the cockpit, too.

The driver uses the steering wheel to turn the boat.

Some cockpits can close and protect the driver inside. The driver wears a type of seatbelt called a harness.

Have you ever done a belly flop? Then you know that falling in water can hurt. Race drivers wear helmets and special suits for protection.

Racing a powerboat takes a lot of skill.

That is why some racers start learning
when they are still in grade school.

Facts about Powerboats

- The fastest powerboats can speed over 200 miles per hour.

- Many powerboat inboard engines are like engines made for cars or trucks.

- Many powerboats aren't used for racing. People use them for fishing, cruising, and waterskiing.

- Some racing boats don't have engines. They use sails and are powered by the wind. Others speed along when people row or paddle.

Types of Powerboat Hulls

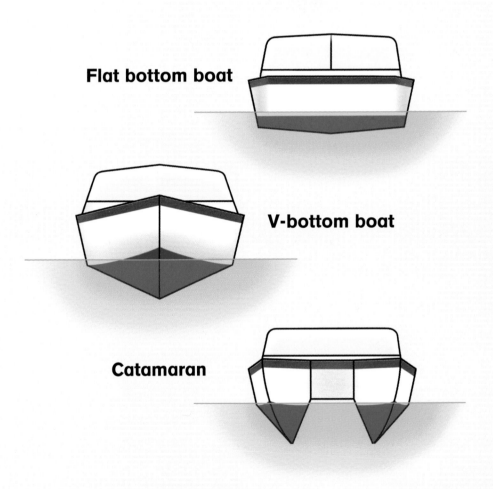

Flat bottom boat

V-bottom boat

Catamaran

Glossary

catamarans: boats with two hulls

cockpit: the place where the driver is

engines: the part of boats that give them power

hull: the body of a boat that moves through water

inboard: an engine built inside a powerboat

outboard: an engine added outside a powerboat

sponsons: parts built on the sides of a boat

throttle: a stick or pedal that controls a boat's speed

Index

About the Author

Lisa Bullard lives in Minnesota, the state they call "The Land of 10,000 Lakes." Ever since she was a little girl she has spent part of every summer swimming and riding in a powerboat at a place called Green Lake. But unfortunately, her family's powerboat isn't nearly as fast as any of the racing powerboats found here! Lisa is the author of nine other books for children, including *Stock Cars* and the award-winning *Trick-or-Treat on Milton Street*.

Photo Acknowledgments

The photographs in this book appear courtesy of: © Tracy Morgan, pp. 3, 12; Roland Dechert, p. 4; Roger Schleicher, pp. 5, 9, 31; © Mark Sharley, pp. 6, 13, 21, 26; © Jim McLaughlin, pp. 7, 8, 17, 18; Brockway Sports Photos, p. 10; Charles Lowrey, p. 11; © Bill Taylor Photography, pp. 14, 15; © Todd Strand/Independent Picture Service, pp. 16, 19, 20, 22; Buzz Miller Photography, p. 23; Tiwana Eastham, p. 24; Leo Schlotter, pp. 25, 27; Illustration on p. 29 by Laura Westlund. Front Cover: Charles Lowrey.